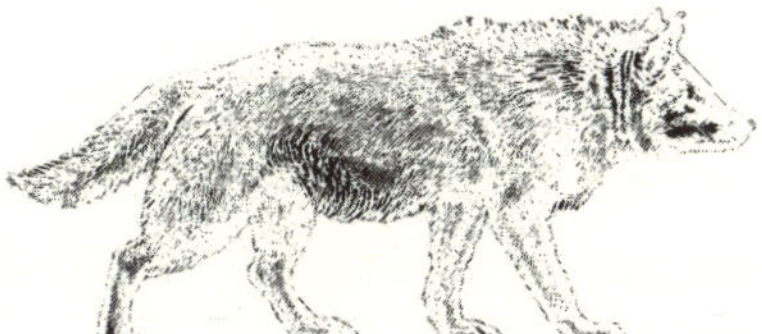

WATER & POWER

Standard Schaefer

June 8, 2005

ISBN: 1-56886-107-9

Design and typesetting: Barbara Maloutas
Back cover photo: Paris Schaefer

Agincourt Press
P.O. Box 1039, Cooper Station
New York, NY 10003
www.agincourtpress.org

TABLE OF CONTENTS

Prologue or Incantation	9
Luster Cross the Mississip	20
The Kid Near Laughlin	21
Convict Lake	22
Another Peak	23
Occidental Express	24
Pony	25
Alcade	26
Sutter's Mill	27
North of Lone Pine, East of Independence	28
Mound	29
Plateau	30
At Lone Pine	31
The Forties or the Mountains No One Talks About	32
Leaving Long Valley	33
Valley	34
Primrose of Los Alamos	35
Independence, California or Mama Tried	36
The Airplane Graveyard of Mojave	38
Hatfied	39
Chavez Ravine or Dodger Stadium, 1948	40
The View from Cal Tech's Jet Propulsion Lab	41
The View from Cal Tech's Jet Propulsion Lab Through CIA Satellite	42
Laurel Canyon	44
Luster and Laurel Griffith Park Observatory	45
Arroyo Seco	46
St. Francis Dam or Mulholland Drive	47
Santa Clara vs. Southern Pacific or How I Came to Love Corporate Personhood	48

The Los Angeles Times' Essay Contest 51
Eaton Canyon 53
Through a Bear Republic 54
L.A.C.M.A. (Concerning the Curator on Horseback) 55
Concerning Allegations of a Ghost 56
Fishing the Ruins: Robinson Jeffers Resurrected 57
On the Porch 58
The L.A. River 59
Desert Inn or Why There Is No Organized Crime in America 60
Blue Mojave 61
Concerning Secession: San Fernando Valley 62
Ranch House 64
Robinson Jeffers in Eagle Rock 65
Café Sunburn Freaks Out 66
Central Avenue: Or That Other West Coast Jazz 67
The Man in the Powder Blue Suit 68
A Report From the Center for the Study of Western Justice. Or the Man in the Powder Blue Suit Addresses the Crowd 70
A Stint in Camarillo or Episodes of the Man in the Window 72
Luster Out of Camarillo on the Way to Tijuana 82
Midland: Or the College of Neglected Science 83

It was the time of the preacher in the year of oh one
And just when you thought it was over, it's only begun.

Willie Nelson, "Red Headed Stranger"

And I say it for myself: the moment I get on one of those sidewalks, I start to fall down.

Emiliano Zapata, December 4, 1912

PROLOGUE OR INCANTATION

Introducing the conclusion of compromise but first
    the slight retracements,
small reversals in pressure and accommodation then a surge of revision
and still you demand a confirmation of the territory, the color, pain
or other moving averages what to some is a three box reversal
the margins more littoral than your need for exegesis when it is
noon and I'm ten grand short, wind at the back, but since
    you're my client
I have to protect you from the banana stabbing your throat
and the ballyhoo of conditions soon to require it, still, there is
the need to address the space and mange that refuses the rhythm
of that lonesome whistle although little attention is paid to the harness
on the wall or big feet in Hot Creek just the denunciations of the page
that only raise the question of the page, but nothing prevents
    an honorable response
to those who refuse to float or the awful taste of chinamen in the water.

10

Unfurling against the sweeping inevitabilities of line, color,
    fear of patterns—

against the far off light hot on the front-matter

eleven weeks of weeds,
                    part formula, part inflection

a twang shreds the strings
to dust and steel
and got penned beneath the needle tedious as the mirror

and hesitating between the purr

    of setting off
toward the hefty light and chunky air

a cold vent in the sequence.

Beneath the robe's dark, salacious swirl

The plane came to a complete stop.
The tower hardly wavered.

In retrospect just a place to rest
the apparatus of absence

memorizing lessons, delivering gifts like
each morning in the baths making a new five-year plan
evening affirming the autonomy of the working class

in sine waves, sand, and over-exposures

but distance is deterrence by other means and at this height, at this angle
lanterns pour out

cogs of dialogue, tin

and scissoring through the misty film

mules in the counting room, goats in the hall

against the propaganda already in place.

A pear off a riverboat sinking out of the lecture
the sound of it split into fourths

stalls the breath the wind lifts a wet sheet the river infused with sloth
as three professors stroll the deck

I have difficulty breathing

three pear shaped professors stroll the deck

a swig of coffee, a word to the professor

the shore is reconciled to eye-level

one foot on the grass the shore up and down swallows lift two feet
resettle six feet in front

a cut or shortness of breath or the riverboat stalls along the shore
a professor puts one foot on the grass

the shore at eye-level three herons rise three feet and resettle six feet
in front, two feet off the ground and stop

I am dazzled by the sound of the grass

you with clarity one further foot out explain the ten thousand miles
all begin at the feet

the professors argue over the correct pronunciation of "Goethe"

the breath stalls the professors resettle on board, the herons two feet
off the ground
are startled by the sound of a pear sinking through water.

dazzled by a shortness of breath, eyes on the grass
I whisper "Goethe" to myself

the sound of a pear sinks through the river.

But you prefer the pulsing, driving, vicarious clarity
to discipline, and precision

to the tea lows where the wrists and finger branch off
into the precise ratio of nails to mud

and for himself a chart of the cave

then a faint depression eludes the digits

he slept in the warm gums of the river,
I prefer the core samples to the words themselves,

a black mass

          rippling through the vent

is sketched back into the circulation of incisions, a crust of sibilance
cut in thirds and filled with saw dust

a whole city designed like a bamboo chair
and accessible only by balloon.

Loud blood types its face.
striations of thunder, no cloud

demure catastrophes

an unfinished symphony of flagging diminuendos, chiseled-off

    but, there is another row of teeth behind these
where we follow the glissando through infinite extensions

past the perishable décor kicking inside the bag
past the dazzle of correct pronunciation

the air being mild and the moon not shinning,
moods filtered by falling.

But, the wind is not the horses it is the moon almost asleep
desert rising in the synapses between all this sunlight
spent studing one's hands

or the hot brace around the legs

stalemate circumstances in an inert precinct

one almost has time to remember why one was leaning on the reservoir,
and staring up at the dam.

The light writes a thousand lines in the rafters, while my hand
slowly wavers over the watermarks

the dove-skinned gloves go on

four lines twelve points and a damp rage
clogs the headwaters

        of the watermarks to come
pressure in the rift and flaws, the glint
stalling along the spine

but out there the light sticks to the exposed corners

birdsong in the west
is only hunger

    in a sentimental mood

despite the ubiquity of pain staring as pain,
metal in the root and a moments notice

but surely it cannot be worthy the moth
flies out the mouth, and twice rounds the head
before bouncing off the light, you so
gruffly interjected

a little attrition, carelessly
                                        sloughed off.

"Our greatest natural resource is the minds of our children."
—Walt Disney

Bride of gunpowder, caviar and benzodiazepines, she said

"Liberty is an elephant swimming to Kansas," her voice

with the French corners cancelled the capricious crag of the sky

but flipping through her eastern pages, exposed corners swirl of leaves

and a constant laying on of the hands—

Through that slit in the attic,

lots and fixed forms
        sleet, crickets

one who plays with marbles
one who conducts a vague science

a slow escalation—
in living only as well as one breaths

against the reclamation of dust, a desert
salvaged from dust by the mildest powders the longest valley
wind through the synapse whispers glimmers dreaming east of Lone Pine

the trees there flutter like porchlights on the grasses of Ohio
were it ever Ohio were there trees
thin as grass if there is any grass left anywhere

in this hopped-up sauna room
on this horse-shaped continent

amid the city born corrupt,
that is to say, capacious.

But I blame moonbeams and a mouse that met on a train
for hiring the man in the powder blue suit, after which
the one with the pen seemed to have the least to do
given his ratio of talent to pillowy cloud, and a rabid anti-socialism
reflected in a nature film about VD and walking off with
    an academy award

even Old Ez watched Uncle Walt whenever he needed too catch up
on some serious foot dangling

but how long can an empire depend on a distracted child
how many hours extra on the exam given the custom
of being born into it and choosing instead to write
not exactly highly selected letters
about the destruction of California long overdue
like relatives and residuals still crawling
off them mountains with a bouquet of bayonet
and penchant for banquets they came down
"to see the elephant"

on this burdened archipelago of bad options and enthusiasm.

LUSTER CROSS THE MISSISSIP

Those who ask shall receive the whites of their eyes
those who hesitate find their thumbs used a bottle stops
the vibrations in the cave are not beginning gods
dark and bent, anointed in fever,
ripples off a lantern following the prisoners
and the sleeper's gleaming along the track
hardly foretell of the octopus to come
only salt grass, rabbit, and miner song, and as of yet
no feel for the furring
or of what only later is hail bop and mutilated jazz
like how this beagle of a century has landed suspect or prospect
to someone before it counting before it someone before it
    someone between
somewhere certainly something was over and what's done is done
but who or what kept on arriving to threaten the inattention
of the gentlemen from nowhere
who stands and states the rights of the accused are primarily
    the rights to their hands
when even a waitress six months from retirement stops on occasion
to smooth out a wrinkle like six months to retirement the hip
finally goes out the river fished with dynamite but what remains
simply remains in streaks and out of respect

THE KID NEAR LAUGHLIN

smells the camel and refused, even up and down a familiar embankment
days without grass no pinch of gunpowder between lip and gum
takes the mind slightly out of range then, howlitzer, thistle, and sump
followed by nights spent swaying on a bar stool until fresh mules,
the names of which he can't recall four ravines ahead three weeks ago
the lips chapped from prayer though he thinks of her mostly
    as three ravines back
and a month between these letters and the seriously lost articles
    of grasshopper
stitched in sunset the elephants drifting behind the hills
ahead or beneath the hull at night down the Colorado up the Gila trail
evenings reading the mule to sleep mornings to find it has strayed
    toward moisture
the clouds of dust over the brambles each morning give poor Betsy away

CONVICT LAKE

millionaires and their lack of convictions even in the time of the preacher
year of oh one ice don't come but urges do a million blown lungs
down some deleted road where the woods never quite come to a point
though occasionally a rattlesnake boot on the road to Christmas
where forests and wilderness go to rest in smaller and smaller transactions
there's a bolt of blue silk that seems to ask do you know the law
    in Inyo County
well, I'm sure you do, and when you see him coming, you just step aside
do what you do but don't interfere glad to oblige and hope you'll stay
but as always the nays seem to have it and there's no one here
    by that name

ANOTHER PEAK

Sluice box, mining car, and bone handled knife—

some points at gunpoint, others wandering a predatory light—

the carbon rubs off on the hands, the dove-skinned
gloves come off,

but having the low forehead, and being from the south, was cold
to form

the lions here are not the typical lions, the light is—

a mess of shadows, chunks of meat
but no fever in the track, just lions of abstraction,
wind and bluff dip their stems in westward bruises

and suck the husks off native insects

deltas and declivities
elevations in scarcity

scramble toward a god so deafeningly plain

but what settles what never quite settles
the flimsiest of substances, the thinnest of odds

still there is this light-guzzling aperture

and an increasing taste for game.

OCCIDENTAL EXPRESS

ten thousand ceilings and this one the last
each ceiling she understands are akin to the others she thinks
each ceiling the same each night the same anger is akin to the others
or attempts to skirt the anger she thinks she knows
the hand of the evening edging the rail she thinks it is
the same distance as the hand before ordinary as
the drought that brings on the distinctions
between herself and the ceiling or the anger staring up at the hand
she thinks she knows or at least those streaks on the bottle
fingers of light wavering on the dresser but small things leave small sighs
and go she thinks she understands the light has to be ordinary
the ten thousandth ceiling demands an ordinary light or drought
she thinks she feels as his legs fail or is dissolved by repetition
the room fills with little rills and ruts of wheel, the light wavers
on the change on the dresser she's come to understand

PONY

a hundred dollar saddle on a twenty dollar horse
a brim of a hat fickle as a compass but what can be done
about all this distance or the strictly singular nature of the trick
especially broke and awaiting a face the obscure numbers
of women staring at the same ceiling same peak each night
another valley until three or four maybe even morning
and again one or two coughing or waving the all clear
a gallon of white dust off Donner Pass on down to Sutter's Mill
even her brother five or six times has come down
to some kind of understanding

ALCALDE

what the tongs are for is the dim and the paper lantern
    irrigates the confusion
between her barbed Spanish and his books encircled in tones
    and contrivance,
but smuggled in through the thief's mouth is what she is careful to keep
of what she's always known and understood of the watch the client
    left on the bureau
the name of the place from where she came some indication
    of the direction
or inclination of the victim's mind she had always believed she'd known
    and understood
though it bothered her at least those six blocks past the *alcalde*
    through the metalworks
exactly where she stands to sell shooting lessons to the chinamen in line

SUTTER'S MILL

and preoccupying the most motionless bodies
is any two stories about the old *vacquero*
who could never entrust anything to memory
noting in his journal that the mind's a ramblin' thing
brought to a bead on a hair scrambled along a ravine
middle of a broiling day, some years before
on a slick place along the decking where he'd found his teeth
in time to get to back to Sutter's Mill or Mormon's Island
for a bite of the white boot now this hot brace around the legs
pitches and rolls the vertebrae a mound of femurs and hollow song
still refusing to take a seat or give up these ceaseless attempts
to get off the blond dunes up off the thin rails
as he sidesteps his way out of a previous estrangement
like higher pay or walking the line, a weakening austerity
in the spastic's movement she thinks she doesn't much mind

NORTH OF LONE PINE, EAST OF INDEPENDENCE

the land leaking from the land dry lightning cut
glass in the sand a nation of almost no imagination
fields an army of engines given only no for an answer
each grain a riddle of error or Nevada but out of Nevada the answer
saw dust in the veins even the *alcalde* is willing to admit
all he remembers is names and dates
nerves of dirt for a sense of direction
but even hurricanes have pangs of property and learned to stay away
out of a healthy regard for the right to stray and nothing is something
    there's plenty of
what leaves as what returns patterns in bone
two or three degrees above sleep or the next valley
where they plant mercury, lead, and arsenic
hope each day the knuckles stiffen a little less
the mouth hardly opens despite centipedes scorpions and Indians
the soft whip of deduction gone drowsily pragmatic
reaches the conclusion—anything with motion has to be wet

MOUND

The appalling thing about Ash Creek is not that its name is Ash Creek
or the big feet at its bank, it's the insistence of the tires to grasp nothing
of wind, sand, and sky—while the hills blow in the dander of a river

brine on the lip, rain rare, but fulfilling leaves no doubt the best
among us
are not fighting the boulders in their eyes any more than we fight
mercury at its lowest

the split belly of a fish—clouds of dust come to cover what was left
of the fish
taken in the weeds, tails sloshing through holes in the knee.

rabbit hopped in hawk's shadow, a rat took a tour of an owl, but
 I'm a practical man
so learn from what's around me the long scissors black coffee
 the pitboss wants
to be rubbed loose the croupier is looking at me for the kelp to close
 the smiler's account
little is mine but this lump of gravy heaving the direction and inclination
 of a claim
what but a lack of water does this moon share with the one above
 why mine
only sage flat, cowbells, streaks of the bottle all day through the valley
for a delivery of ice and a burr to keep the lice off
the room today four inches lower than before, still I don't plant
I go to bed early, ice or not, and for a pint of blood, or half a bottle
 of whiskey
you get the deed to lie of the land, I'd get to Carolina in my time

AT LONE PINE

the same grudge each sky the bottle drops the flies scatter
and still the *alcalde* can't say how much justice is need or want
brings these sparrows to the gravel whether it's Independence
or simply a Mormon claim still insists between the levels of sentiment
and the rates of violent crime citing the bald spot who can't prove it
not for them marbles or those beans baked into bracelets
of day and night poured through until there's no eye
to revise the fuss and rumors of rime

THE FORTIES OR THE MOUNTAINS NO ONE TALKS ABOUT

begins or does not at forty or in the movies
with or without gold or legal age whether or not war
is work for all always with Diamond Lil there is work
her falsetto heels across the floorboards
Spanish trickling from the dais a kind of provocation to
the violin gradually consuming the lanai or a climate
built on gunpowder and smeared over the eyes like Rita Hayworth
high on velvet or was that the girl printed in the background of the check
who leased her eyes to the city of Ojai
or perhaps it was another Miranda altogether
who true to the rites of spring took her guns strictly bullets first
and from there was shipped east and west at once
by Colonel Capra and the Hollywood Canteen
to cough out an alibi no brighter or better than Ojai
or Odessa, daisy after daisy the sky black with ducks
when Disney against the metaphysics asked to sit this one out
in Casablanca like a brand of beer like troutfat and hard freight
    like minor song
brought out to defeat more recent arrivals such as twelve-tone music
and a cresting fluorescence concealed and embodied in the punch-line
to the fishing guide's joke that he don't mind reading
but only for knowledge the valley returning to its
lush sheep-like devastation relies very sparingly on the reel
or Veronica Lake and opening day but knows damn well
that with an airport this town could be as big as Laredo
so is willing to abide questions and interviews that all boil down
to whether or not he is impotent but the only way to avoid impotence,
sincerity or Hollywood, as Stravinsky said, is to live there once and for all

LEAVING LONG VALLEY

Banjo ripples in the chain link fence
fiddlescrape in the run off
barbed wire to straighten the teeth

birds flit through the gash in the attic, and emerging endlessly
from a meeting with refusal— the deep, gleaming
pawned off things

churns a catfish music
up on blushing rock, Benton's Crossing the caddis wakes up
wake up, my darling, go and get your gun you know I haven't the heart
for those who in their turn will turn and leave
maybe toward Olancha on the way to the Zion
of rising earlier and taking more breaths
always eager to fight the boulders in their eyes

while I stir the morning broth—
apple's blush, shadow of crow

the hope today all this rattling
looses maybe a barrel of rain

value, no, valor

makes a very faint sign.

VALLEY

Through the heat lamps and the chaparral past Manzanar
hostages of mapwork and opening days the mirage
is ground to a glass of tap

                        refined later and brought recently
to this side of the Sierras in the belly of a fish despite
the drop in defense contracts and teenage pregnancy
a rise in I. Q. scores to the mid-nineteen-seventies
and the snow-boarders's fear of public transportation

each year there is seventy percent less snow pack, more rain coming
like anti-venom and precision chair-lifts the repeated introductions
of earthworms to rainbow trout with no water rights whatsoever
and without a place for rest, and sunk in the guts, a gust
of an afternoon almost divine in its emptiness, almost brittle,
the dry light in this crater makes the moon stagger all morning
toward two holes in the head.

PRIMROSE OF LOS ALAMOS

came out wild and lonely like Manzanar the cobra opened its kimono
to swallow the *caliche* of an evening boiled in torn flowers, but virtue
 is what remains intact
an equation of days shorter and more exact walking absently through
eyes for the deaf, ears for the blind and the constant attempts
 to surrender
no more audible than the gizmos of heat and formaldehyde,
 the hard math
of photographs from Los Alamos the MP holding a sack of rattlesnakes
 over a crater
as the sky roseblack spun forward just not forward enough to close
 out the crickets
deleting the moon or mother's preoccupation with pruning until
 there is no primrose
in the desert no repeated attempts to surrender just father's habit of
 shifting his weight through a sand colored kitchen mother had
 dreamed of since New Mexico
where today, remarkably, a bird is singing, just bearably, maybe virtue
is what is just bearable after the extreme tides of inertia, gold like ice caps
melting from our fillings while the barbed wire with its long division
invokes the Medusa solution, for high tides and irredeemable desert—
nuclear winter though here even the English Department and
 the Gaming Commission
are ardently opposed

INDEPENDENCE, CALIFORNIA OR MAMA TRIED
(AFTER AND ABOUT MARY AUSTIN)

Mother says we must not speak appreciatively about landscape
    and flowers
especially to boys who don't like and can't forgive the habits
    of frisk-tailed critters
they constantly pursue down a three-mile egg up the round, blunt hill
    they envy
heaving west and drowsy toward the Sierra, south from Panamint
    and Armagosa
west and south many an uncounted, colicky day followed by
    those instincts
known as branding, but Mary there's not much more to love than
    standing in the doorway
or a three-legged man with his simple edginess traced in alkali
    with slight saline deposits
on a bowl where the lake had been now we're luck to have hound dogs
    at the border
so rarely catching the tune of so many winters or writers fabulously
    abrupt
in their failure to slough off the habit of talking to creatures they don't
    care to understand
but little hoot owl little hoot owl don't be offended how the wind
    calls roll
of yours or anyone afflictions or how dogs lick the face of
    their natural prey
or do you, like Mama, believe ignorance sooner or later dies
    of fatigue and
settles against what the balloon-framed house never delivers the sediment
just keeps on arising like a rose in misty old England some moral essay
that never got this far west perhaps it is only the hustle of heather around
    a borax marsh
makes the wickiups not rattle and the snakes not even bother to coil
so few have the patience to strike even where expected given that the hot
    sink is in

and the brackish pools south toward oddly cattier climates seem
to raise little
more than the scantest imagination until there is little need to work or
even be comfortable
the pipe no longer need be secret, and to get out you simply uninstall
the rodent
from the brain stem or tie your daughter to the chair and type but Mary,
you have to learn to trust something even the tedious emptiness that
disclose the divine
and it doesn't hurt to learn to fish, or at least remember Mother's dictum
of catch and release.

THE AIRPLANE GRAVEYARD OF MOJAVE

Fat on suicides and cluttered with lead balloons
the kiss-my-axle hurly burly of flies not rising
from blocks of light, knots of mirage siphoning off
the sound of muffled bees reminds the director
of certain eastern spiders but ever buoyant rarely embarrassed
the cadavers in the voting box cast shadows on the concrete
and concrete keeps coming hard in such heat
the heat keeps still and the fat keeping voting the dead.

HATFIELD

Another overheated syllable with one arm thunder
the other a boulder or gnashing teeth and thunder clasp
the sapphire always in the mind moths staring the stars down
from the roof renders the oracle from muscle, guts and luck
on the part of a tray of chemicals, blue dog licking his teeth
as the fleas are on their way out, he leans on a shovel and diligently hums
against the saline stains in the sag of the porch, balcony light retracting
from the riff raff and rafters more will than sensitivity
in a very fine, very lucrative ash.

CHAVEZ RAVINE OR DODGER STADIUM, 1948

That the sunset is sublime but the men are not seems no response
to the singsong girls sneering at the tooth still quivering in the prey
all the private dicks in the city cannot refute that beauty depends
first on the fundamental dishonesty of the victim though
tonight boys, we pick 'em up for everything the plot like the hasty reply
 of the fence
must not sleep through the gradual invention of Israel
and the string bikini the failure of Potdam and Truman's resurrection
no more riveting than the agenda slept off in a stadium
and who can refute the addenda of parrots with their southern accents
stumbling in like the rent three days from innovations like a foreclosure
like slant drilled wells and a surplus of refineries like the instinct
 toward not looking
or the lousy tango on the part of the physicist who testified that density
 and suggestion
is only as promiscuous as the fungus bleaching out this side of the valley
is easily suppressed on the part of the voices, surging in pieces.

THE VIEW FROM CAL TECH'S JET PROPULSION LAB

Parvenus drunk on the rum of resurgence or what was possibly oxygen,
seven dollars a week five days of rations and a rifle you can keep—
brings the coins that spins the contagion

but Circler of Circles, there is no north
or south in space
    only fever through the wire and a murmur between the rails
the clack or crank of the wheel against our heritage of howlitzer
    and horseback
whose ghosts now slosh through the back ground radiation, as if
rain then intuition, sparingly distributed, could suffocate the jar
    full of frogs
before the shoes dry and the world with its conditions, like art or
    poetry, is best left
to others

or sunken in the chest, a glass pump

and for fuel, the alleged force of beautiful things,

measured in feathers at then end of a gasket.

THE VIEW FROM THE JET PROPULSION LAB THROUGH CIA SATELLITE

Hail bop, a floss-like light strobes the yolks—

photons and placebos eating the placenta of outerspace
seem almost dignified against the kiss-my-ass hoodoo of desperadoes
who whupped the Filipino who got high on flower ballads
now standing on the shoulders of viruses
until they regain their chilling, technical virtues—

pattern, mask, and ape

    but against the precise ratio of nails to mud, a hole in the proof
that September like Chile was full of irrational numbers
derived from algebra, Kabala and the bell raining math.

Counter-information polishes the congestion
of assertions and disclosures redistributed
between the gizmos of instinct and the dogs trained
to do instinct for them, when counting backward
and crawling toward the bikini of God.

But even Brecht on occasion got his girl to Mulholland on occasion
where in the name of Galileo they counted the stars and when no
    stars came
to be counted they counted the freeways

either way they got the same number of syllables
    and when the syllables lost their policy making position.

They drank to the damnation of Newton
with an over-the-counter accuracy Newton would only quantify.

    Even anger was on the borrow, and perhaps it was not space

we had needed, just a self-sustaining cylinder of light
declarations of simplicity, episodes of sidewalk
arch door stuck

    in the fresh, young paradigms so eager
to zip and unzip their complete lack

of a practical application

        that brings the dopey snake to a boil
and evaporates the last of this dancing water, that all night battered
the abstract lawn.

LAUREL CANYON

Beautiful first then commonly agreed upon, stress echoes and e.k.g.s
days in chambers meted and metered in drops and dribbles
of whoever's suede whoever stays, all heart, like the market rising
the wife reaching for a dress of another color for another result
the oceans are not memories geographies not patterns
the ceiling swollen with two or three hours that almost failed to meet
in the closet of a city structured like a gift boutique
simple music is bred from an offensive lack of maintenance
elegant old ladies simply unwilling to work
for a solid, if barely committed supposal but who
took the longest to leave? who the skin, light, French door?
all that was left of the man in the window was the sip of occasion
years spend practicing to play once and die for the sky line
receding redemptions preemptions a suite of rooms along the ridge of pie.

LUSTER AND LAUREL
GRIFFITH PARK OBSERVATORY

The same grudge each sky
two lungs of Styrofoam and a large egg
but with a white necktie and a cutaway coat
the wolf snows broken teeth

the beagle in the peptide chain
broke loose during a lecture
on the birth of the galaxy

and enthused about a tight little plus sign
formerly of feeding and flight

infused himself with grout

a dinner of olives
and lemon wandering the aisles

the owl in his chest
east and sharp as a K

dust, blanched and divided

she said, "Howdie, Ranger. Here's my library card."

they order the tomatoes in oil

he didn't even try to understand
he read the subtitles

turned the wheel and pulled the crank
the frogs suffocated but the shoes were at last dry.

ARROYO SECO

Like the blacksmith who got rich on Chinese helmets, puny water
and its priest-like task looks awfully fatal as it banks
and proceeds out of sight but to this day the hedges
the oily film through exhausted dams and letters to the editor
about the swimming pools we deserve or at least this one vein
we're gonna keep, green blue, no, blue magnesium, manzanita humming
autumn ice on the gate maybe once a year, bilge in the pump
    nails snowing
through the turbines up on blushing rock where fish and game
once incorporated now inflamed with heavy cable and lunar clarity
twisting dry the same towel to save some time damned as we do
damned as we can't even imagine the primrose, sandhill crane
or another mosaic of battered prose born from friction seeping the itch
of what was previously an old man now dismantled like clean air
or suddenly crossing and recrossing the weeds of a fathomless silence
that has long since raised a stick to fend or feed off the dogs.

ST. FRANCIS DAM OR MULHOLLAND DRIVE

After the first there is no other only fussy months on the periphery
of a constant, if unflappable pressure, and a diversion of pressure
toward afflictions of intemperance,

really just this one segment
one level of dimness for one level of density applies the peacock
to sleep off the celery

but a bright, bubbly feeling is confused with envy
for the dead then this current drop in pressure
invites another set of fingers to the crack in the bread
crumbs to the ducks she thinks he engineered,

the minute, careful exclusions
surfacing occasionally like worms in the diagram
metal and grout, then a rock in the eye

but in these moments of resistance even the rain seems
to get through only by knowing the officer on duty
big dog licking his hand, bread under the arm
each morning to his former office the old ditch-tender
to himself thinks *after the first there is no other*,

just the journalist who gave him the phrase
and died alone

waiting for the plumber or anger to arrive.

SANTA CLARA VS. SOUTHERN PACIFIC OR HOW I CAME TO LOVE CORPORATE PERSONHOOD

(*for Stapp Beeton*)

The beast trapped in a cat's cry, six alarm other thing done this time
without fighting his breath doused in Fire Chief the flames finding the
green, wet wood
just as the couple hears themselves through the other side of the wall
again
the clerical error is affirmed that distance or nearness is deterrence
seems to strangle the instincts' aesthetics and four thousand years
of privatization
culminates in the headnotes of a previous decision—tautology
slanders fatigue

and even the bird song lacks volition like the paunch of sky the
next morning, a tongue
hung backwards, kindly the gutterhum of August surrounds the legs
of the court reporter
who blames the excessive heat on his damn thirst
the word property evaporates from the dossier
the word slavery not even noted
and yet if this contraption belongs to the shareholders
and yet if this contraption stands and speaks
but in a frontier built on slotting fees, without inventory and
with no signs of being right all along
just a tide, a moon, dispute and dictation
then smokestacks lightning toot toot
the legacy of stirrups goes mist wild with parrots, patents and
statistical behavior
into the headlights of an octopus at the start of its garrulous rise
the hard-won heretofore argued back from the refunds of rigor
finds its remainders in a voting box full of cadavers now a dollar movie
twitching through a primate half asleep and head over heels to
the ends of the earth
bunkhouse after bunkhouse following the blinking hand

through grasslands, scholarship, and a snarl of refineries
until what seemed an amendment to the purposed jurisdiction
is rendered coyly near extinction in a felicitous report
that there will never be any end to the free gifts
or the current resurgence in watching your back.

•

Whether poverty is granted personhood, there is always exile, said Said
a kind of paradise built on the clones of nuance like scrutiny or biotech
they acquire a chin just to get shot up in Los Gatos, Tehacapa Pass
    or the Ottomans
sometimes in a B movie that isn't quite false given the number
    of metaphors
that sleep with their victims given putting greens in the national forest
and the water stolen to get it there.

But between meaninglessness and suffering, better to number
    the questions
like how long the chauffer been swaying gaudily from the ceiling
or do you prefer frog-gigging to carelessness or the coming world
about which, it has been said, it is furnished exactly as this one
three days for the IRS, four with nothing to drink
until the dog's analysis makes more sense than another day of stillness
hauled ecstatic from the snub-nosed syllables and an unwillingness
    to work.

•

Chaos is the receptor of almost democratic impulses thunder
    cannot extract
the fuel from the vertebrae of the heathen Chinese who have no more
    to drink
than a lack of rain, stirred with a nail, says the chauffer who art

so if you need roots, I suggest rancor, disaster, willful exaggeration
even vindictiveness

over gnosis, luminescence, and an exceptional climate.

Heaven is where we go to settle strictly older scores, but nothing is
left of heaven
save the remarks of the plaintiff.

In exile, there is nothing but shoulders
an ache that explains nothing

no different than the dog's seizures that seems to say
the leadership has come down
to say a few words

start—run—reg—edit take a bath the lights not on
not gonna play your goddam games
I'm different and don't care who knows it, our father in the station shouts

where's my angry young man?

THE LOS ANGELES TIMES' ESSAY CONTEST

All civilization develops first as conspiracy, than as agriculture,
  finally paradox
the bruise that stays bruised hires the rich thus competition is eliminated
between stacks of documents and their standard deviations, roosters
tear the night apart and stop, only to take credit for the appearance
  of the sun
but here we deal directly with the department of the interior
which today grants a slide or flood another slow fall of wet checks,
muffled temblors
          that seem to fan out from the epicenter
  of the ingénues'
remark—Hollywood is just gorges, she said over breakfast one speedboat
  at a time
sudden as a run in her stocking she almost fails to mention to
  the officer on duty
that each day it only get easier to face the mountain lions on
  Chavez Ravine
or the loose type wandering the street but who can refute the
  ingénue' song
when its any pew in a saloon ad the doubloons of applause have been
  squandered
on another forced confession another freshly baked marriage turned
  impeccably cruel
coincident with the fire on the eve of the election
that killed the first socialist mayor just as sure as Jupiter rising
  over Tikabu Peak
or the requests for the honor of the ice-worm's absence, any bank holiday
  of his choice,
not to mention president Lincoln's perpetual buffet the opening of
  Madam Tussaud's
North Hollywood San Fernando but on the hill behind twenty windows
away from the stench of oil, crime is only business by other means
hence the ballet set for strictly younger elephants
or so many postcards mailed at once from the final three-thousand feet

of a baked Alaska not even Otis Chandler could eat,
given the indecency of having to address the crowd
and the embarrassing struggle against his own man in the street.

EATON CANYON

Rude stove morning's horn maybe today a little moisture
in the factory smoke the grid lock of discretion or the inscrutable orchid
thirteen bolts out of fifty-two, twenty-seven
brushed metal knobs until the towels are dry or a seven-letter word
for not even an hour postman setting off the dogs and her
 daughter's letter
to practice Italian limited largely to her mother's name Leena after Leena
rules out Nevada and rubs the mineral against her foot thinking
this I got to persevere still preoccupied by California or a semester
 of dust
argued back from the waist and from the waist up she's strictly
 old fashioned
Leena after Leena to be drunk on E. Line Street seems no excuse
for dedicating this brushed metal to a girl who never crossed the line
at least with the poor ones its early to rise all day inside the typewriter
 ten fingers,
ten methods excluded though endurance though often precision
 gets results
it is rarely inauthentic especially the levers or carefully carrying by hand
the perfectly columned repetition of carriage and lever
reaches the keys and begins again with the lever in the throat
but maybe this time it blows over before it unfairly compares
Leena with her harp busting through the vest or a Mother's concern
winnowed down to mother-of-pearl.

THROUGH A BEAR REPUBLIC

for PS

Concerning love in the frontier the call of the wild
seems strictly an amateur's song the melody of eccentrics whose
    sense of timing
has never been established though the clock in the center of town
    still ticks
the arms are nowhere to be found but little good has come from
    metaphor, symbol or Nevada only another infuriating set of figures
    brings any two together whether
in the name of carpool lanes or an irrational devotion to survival,
as the book of Mormon says, whatever survives must be marriage
the rest is banjo, debt, and hysteria particularly in the eyes of
    the saloon owner
who finally reconciles himself to our newfound temperance represented
    today
in the signature on the bottom of a bowl flutes of champagne
tomorrow the squeal of fighter jets and an army corps of engineers
attempts to remove the scent of squawfish from the magnolias
but inhaling the spores we come to eyelevel the Comanch
and their notion of beauty as a hungry coyote
who on occasion refuses the extravagance of carrion
but who can refuse the extravagance of coyotes
given the boom in parade permits and the bust in petting parties
leading blessedly to surrender blessed too are the abandoned mines,
the surrender of the bible salesman at our neighbor's door
but blessed most are they who found their saloons on big rocks
    and wild fire,
for they shall know marriage not as hunger nor as ornament—but as
    a distillation—
what the late Shoshone say Nothing is more loyal or more febrile than a
    family of wolves
or two hearts that howl in unison maybe only the flourishing of this bare
    and blundering love
can annihilate the unbound feeling that comes from being prepared.

L.A.C.M.A. (Concerning the Curator on Horseback)

The sluice box and bone-handled knife come to blue space,
white box I could see the fur was bark, and the dust brought
the hogs to the surface, a slight starlight beneath the forehead
engraved the brush fires in modulated hymns, spring
in strobes we welcomed the bluff and all at once
the avant-garde arrived with light mints to argue hard
and promiscuous the names and dates already a museum
enlightenment even in fragments replaced real estate
more pragmatic than the curator's rare statement but
the record showed there was no light made of mint
unless one means it wasn't very heavy— it wasn't, more like
    a refrain which
they would not— furiously enlightenment traveled toward us
furiously no one was paying attention to who asked the question
who answers only the blot of a city, eating its placenta
angles more local where abstract the same way
traffic traffics in possibility, we were like Europeans
could not resist the little rocks or fuzzy drinks so
often mistaken for admiration because no one wanted
to ever be alone, like Europeans,
but August in Europe is part-time and if retirement were such
    a good idea,
surely the curator would have done it by now
because where nothing grows nothing accrues any interest,
and we must be like Europeans only with Georgia on our minds.

CONCERNING ALLEGATIONS OF A GHOST

doors go out light and the floor goes up
curtains darken the boards a door opens steps go down
an inherent unevenness but into the cold spot walks the light
a wall in the equation curbs the floor the tilt
of an agreement corners the dark spot in the corner
two walls and a knob in hand the hand in beveled light
goes right past the cheek and a rib in the wall the door opens
the place is gone the ribs are everywhere and happy to do it,
glad to oblige but please stay seated, the light is only passing through
to face a cold spot in the curtains and close the door behind you
are welcome to the back of the light the grin in your face goes out
light suspirations broad sheets of water walk right through
the power and apparition conduits and conditions, streaks
are the least of the floorboards the dead are the real reformers
the last set of curtains guileful as formaldehyde climbs what's left
of the place
where there is no place, just ruffling of ground against shade,
shale, exhaust

FISHING THE RUINS: ROBINSON JEFFERS RESURRECTED

I am tired of every day deities like supply and demand,
I envy the wolf
even with blood in its urine, at least is seems to reassure him
he won't waste his life revising what he himself doesn't like

like the photograph of the MP standing on the platform
beneath the checkpoint and the tower no more black
and white orchids in the Catalpa trees
put them all in the sack of rattlesnakes the MP is holding
and pull out the head of Medusa
from Joaquin Murieta, tell it—

the only diamonds we shall hold will be born in our bowels
the legacy of stirrups and confidence intervals
normally distributed down a steep road built on gambling dragons
and ammonia

where chinamen
is one word, power outages
are an invention imported from Texas
the best candidate's slogan is "Have you know shame?"

and if Tokyo surrenders in advance
we will hear nothing of it because when we're alone
we prefer to be by ourselves like the ingénue leaning on the retired cop
who pilots his own plane, always staring at the forgeries of the ravine,
the false purgatories where we will make no more great joy
with your or anyone's bodies

and still for you, I have only a very short list
of things to fix—

Not even the flies hovering
over you are on it.

ON THE PORCH

what won't quite grasp the glint at the back of the mouth
of the alleged rapist next door to the dentist or
the linguist who fancies himself a bit of poet when far verse
is bourbon for breakfast or worse the young at art
high on gorgeous but empty disallusionment
come out wind through dull pupils, the right full
of light, left full of motion days spent falling down
palms burning the hair off the city as it
complains about chronic pain to the swaybacks
the double-hipped the constant attempts
to avoid tying the fly to a string which
somehow bolsters the image of finality
that starts at the thigh and ends at the starched white sheet
worn casually around the neck of a screenwriter
who insisted it had always only been personal
this side of Chavez Ravine

THE L.A. RIVER

smog typhoid celery like a ghost splashing out of a beaker
comes a dot off the ridge to cancel the orthography of
bramble and pine the abyss fits in the parenthesis
fragrance of isotherms route numbers and the glint of chrome
that hits the vein each day more prophylactic
than the exit wound of pragmatism and public work but with a
    plush silence
has no preference though if pushed hedges with performance
dim pleats in the slovenly limits of custom, obligation, and verve
works the work of the major languish against slober, skin,
and any serviceable language of submission and proposal
come and gone in spars and shafts part e-flat part pleas
twelve chords of gray ash until sixty watts off shore,
it does nothing, but at least it does it consistently, despite shortness
of breath and the liver's long career of whispering yes

DESERT INN OR WHY THERE IS NO ORGANIZED CRIME IN AMERICA

another hatchback turns up in Tijuana Hoover takes the call
but how long will the nation be saved by car thieves
or window washers wiretapping the former child star
this one hired for his resemblance to Howard the Huge
takes a crack from a chair, but stumbles back in
to throw off the call-girls moonlighting as process servers
or to put the presto into the Negro's mite-sized heart
and sup the vapors off a vixen pouting in the lobby
eyes no less sharp than a ball of wool, steel blue
to maintain the illusion that poor Howard could ever fuck at all
though who could deny the sincerity of the denial
given the transfusions pure as a sealed room
phone ringing thirty floors up blue spike of television
scrubbing the eyes out as poor Howard no codeine
is asked to forgive the absence of procedure on the part of
the part of the Pentagon, the wrong aircraft buzzing his room
but in such an electric environment who can lament
the streakiness of subpoenas that never quite stick

BLUE MOJAVE

Off the back and out the echo after the bluff, moving through
 the celery bog
to the big sink, past all the refineries of this afternoon drones of the next
but up with the wand forward with whiskey
the robe makes one further slouch,

the plank
comes and goes, fuming

then curtain after curtain of assertions and disclosures, a stretch
 with wiggle
delivered with the utmost discretion, like the rack left bare
when the prize winner is in remission, and the dead have lost
 all confidence—

the ocean is only a phonetic corruption
of whatever formlessness the Shoshone say only a wolverine would have
 a word for

laughter mauls a palsied code
artless tessellations improvised in rock
and bone, until all comparisons learn to sit still

and be appropriate.

There is something immune to salvation, balanced on rumors of
 a fulcrum,
it lets loose its slack fugue—

an insatiable appetite for shell fish, sine waves
not quite wavering not quite nowhere
not quite with no where left to go.

CONCERNING SECESSION: SAN FERNANDO VALLEY

Hard corn and raw tautology, and pumping through the pleasure panels
a light, golden oil across a pornographic veneer—

asserts the only good metaphor is a dead one, for example, the
    screenwriter
in residence

turns again to the night before, Rome burning in a very old book
while he slept

then first things first: launch the satellites
and a horse's ass hallelujah to how long it takes
the knee to unlock or the waitress to take his order

but something leaps out of the puddle he has for a heart
and he's on the river with the rod no later than ten
with a hangover in the form of a question
like what's the ugliest part of your body?

Some say it your mind, but almost as if on the cliff of a yawn the mind
    drifts out of season
the robe falls to the syrup some call a river

and for a sense of place I suggest absence of body

maybe Debbie is kind enough to come along
you'll need a clean garage and plenty of lettuce
rain like exercise

loses it glamour and gets more exciting

because if you're not from here then you're almost certain to belong
among the ooze of detail at the backend of a room

you just have to go back in
for another bout in the pouting den

wind up walking all day across a long room full of shoes still on order
but you could really go unnoticed
nothing here goes to waste.

RANCH HOUSE

for PV

beyond where and when and under what conditions
or the blunt volume that ekes across what is left of a very spare room
is the mountains no one talks about even as the walls do swagger
and once again dancing for a living when the revolutionary spirit entered
    the snack bar
an obscene choreography of ants lured across the plates
and a renewed interest in chance, just for the chance to feel better
than the bald spot who can't help but tell us
how much we know nothing and why the struggle to explain
who we live off and under what conditions
we refuse to theorize the languish— raw flax and pure contemplation
seem to muffle self-hatred and its twin, though both sides of the sierras
have their supporters, there's no ether where none intended
despite the parenthesis or something the alleged publisher requested
his lips moving something he hoped to drink from our skulls
though the minute, careful exclusions in our own lean presence
hardly unsettle the puddle we share for a heart, no fish leaping
in my dreams or yours, just hinges and reactions that smoke the river
and the weave of pipe and broken glass against the blur of the lamp,
carp sluring forth a drab wall against our blunt if bare-foot hostility
because you and I know the exile-in-reverse is a comic genius
with a white necktie and a cutaway coat, he keeps on accepting
the limits to our exceptions, the one tenacious cave, gun metal gray,
and though the water rises, the gasper goo has flashed its tail—
we ease through the gruel to get to the resilience, and for one day only
do exactly as we please

ROBINSON JEFFERS IN EAGLE ROCK

Concerning the dim notion of afterlife afforded the natives introduces
the first of many indigenous insults, but what exactly did the translators
mean by "bold" "evolve" "evoke" what bold is in these arroyos but a
rock balancing on the tip of a prestigious collage and why the
balloon refuses to rise over the taco truck

or out of college a refusal to form an opinion even when furnished with
the obligation
to be polite during certain successful misunderstandings

about the momentum of refusal and the end of local knowledge when
what absorbs the verge is the big spaces at the end of a revolver
analogous to the vague craft of infusing documents with helplessness
or onto a lack of documents the inconspicuous promotion of the poor
given the accusation that "the why is missing" from the upholstery

but on those who would weave paradise for a sect so forth and some such
ought not to be said

care instead spent on distinguishing between native and wild
always akin to anger, squandered so often on tiers or the mist laden
metaphor of wife
gone stagnant on balled up love, trips to the beach—harsh as
the territory
of supposal the outpost's overused underfed mules of amusement—
though I very nearly saw her with her hat off—the repulsive frenzy
of autobiography
scattered amid the sediment of libraries wadded up and stuffed in
the mouth
of the translator who'd made every sincere attempt to disable the device.

CAFÉ SUNBURN FREAKS OUT

The way I see it Barry, you're obviously a man with a profound sense of justice who understands the value of a musical education, but this is the land of silk and money, so by now you've realized you've only been sold the climate, whereupon, as they say, the oven shuts violently. I can see the seepage in your heart. That comes from selflessness, and selflessness leaves guys like us somewhat unsatisfied. That's why if you're willing to try, I'll set aside all my other affairs and devote my attention strictly to you. These are not insurmountable ampersands. They're cherished inexcusables. So, I won't have you going round calling us criminals. Guys like us are worse than criminals, Barry. We live off crooked dough and don't even do our own stealing. But before you cruise off for burgers, I want you to understand the doll I got is thirsty and takes it personal if she isn't acquitted an ocean view. She has that unbound feeling that comes from being prepared. And as you know, I myself have devoured a headboard or two. That's why I don't want you smoking in pajamas or trying to think this thing through. I know you believe work will redeem us, but that's cause your waxy. You lost your fusebox simmering so long on the low blue flame. But this is louie louie and I got the hidie hidie ho. The only thing that keeps us going are the preposterous odds we'll find any undertaking more unworthy. All the integrity in the world can't keep us from singing our nocturne three lanes thick, twice the limit and grocking the sopping pink.

CENTRAL AVENUE: OR THAT OTHER WEST COAST JAZZ

That they don't make Jews like Jesus seems to cancel the dancing
but with them that brung ya there is never coincidence only victims
peppered with trumpets, thinks the officer on duty who has
come to believe
coincidence should work compositionally, especially if work is to
redeem us
assuming the hose don't freeze and the brooding bat gets set loose
in the sax
as long as he doesn't get tapped out below the stairwell by the
abrasive hush
of some fine white lady talking lit-ra-char saying "process is the nigger
of technique"
and what did she mean her favorite poem was Sun Tzu's Art of War
and going on about some road named Jack that went to New York to
suck off Gore Vidal
and why Jack try to talk above the music there is nothing above
the music,
it's bats all the way up, a few truffles, caviar, integrated schools, mama's
little baby
knows the real money is not in dancing but in slant drilling and
offset wells,
most of all it is the refinery certainly not in due process the
latest contagion
like United Artists or rolling black outs like Uncle Remus dialing
homicide
as he should and knows he ought to say he didn't kill that white woman
but he certainly didn't miss her snoring, as he backed out the drive,
so careful
to put the hard bop to the jockey on the lawn.

THE MAN IN THE POWDER BLUE SUIT

dandy lions bobbysocking off Laurel Canyon think"kinky" is British
for tilted
and"how do you like you often?" as the woman later named Laurel
though often he doesn't, often he does always another pint to
the Gulliver
and a single lime to brush the teeth

she's three miles all mountain, but he approaches as an equal, almost an
honorable man
because someone somewhere is in need of assistance
because the first time is forever and of course, dear Contempt
because detailed accounts lead to further doubt
nothing to go on but bandaged rain throbbing in the hands

until who can blame the detectives their division of detection
into three hinky parts the first where you don't get up, gentlemen,
I'm only passing through the second blacked out beneath the stairwell,
increasingly shallow but jumping to no conclusion the third
and most vestigial buried in a cigar box and gradually wrapped up
in papers
no one is willing to sign the fourth is thirty years of dredged sleep
and public service only ditch-tenders and prospectors remain solvent
not even the cigar girl parrot coughing on her shoulder
offers any assurance beyond one vast set of cracks on the lip
the sting of not a drop or dribble though the dam spills blood orange
occasionally

and on occasion a kiss from the bride
in exchange for coincidence, intuition, and clues withheld
otherwise moderation seeks the occasion, even if sparingly,
in regard to hypnosis, ghosts, and psychics

but by now the concierge can see the steady hand of false routine
how vast and empty the overbearing will of the place since the upturn

in relics
the upstart vicissitudes means every effort must be made to collect from
the high window
or "the muse of integrity" already ground down to agendas
and procedures
sometimes only the count or the movement of the count through the
cold shoulder
to the dent gone tepid always against another puddle of curtains
observation makes an awkward imitation of one degree two
degrees closer to getting stronger all the time

A REPORT FROM THE CENTER FOR THE STUDY OF WESTERN JUSTICE

OR THE MAN IN THE POWDER BLUE SUIT ADDRESSES THE CROWD

Justice even if improvised requires a theory of leisure, malaria, depletion but inclinations toward geographical upheaval keep the matter to half a page give aridity of certain extractions, desalizations, and a taste for exploit given that the avant-garde is represented by a bramble of contents, for example oowa oowa oo, Betty Blue got a new Declaration of Independence and California crossed a long room of the shoes still on order turn her big eyes out to sea. But night is not a ride on a seal and revolution is not taking your clothes off. Chaos like the octopus of history is always a last resort—the slope blanco of unauthorized collaborations between nature and experience because ambience is the killer ap— not language or the octopus eating from your hand.

For example, the word "evoke" as it evaporates in a wind gone drowsy but what has happened here is that the desert got out of the car climbed into the trunk; the saloon keeper and the speculator colluded to cancel the lecture on "events"; the desert announced a final shower of arrows and hatchets to cancel the whimsy of coyotes swimming their fleas off, flies in the buttermilk, moths in the sleeve, fused sand— until today, the sheriff seems suddenly old-fashioned and usury is art given a renewed interest in chance, like the California condor which—strictly speaking— is only a dinosaur, of late, in resurgence unlike wisdom or beauty or candor, advocacy is a bitter nostrum that depends on no one is listening and balanced by an all-out drought— the usual enactments like swearing off the fly or higher pay, undermine all efforts to organize, even around a fog, especially given the vantage from within the amber, where like a rich kid who has no face, only a West Point chin and a love of puns, ridicule serves the property of visibility as a kind of subsidy to raw incorporation, only the rise of camping the immigration of Harvard drop-outs, cut-throat trout, vegetarians, and the Kiwanis—could diminish at least the visibility of property, provided vegetarian is the rural pronunciation for "bad shot," and temptation is the better part of intent, the side effect of fence laws, trains full of river water delivered to those who would not clamor toward Cíbola or el Diablo simply out of the way it sounds, although who can fault the insistence on the part of the jeweler that he be paid for his time, despite how unproductive the claim that between any two points there is a Texas or a place where the landscapes hang, even grace—cannot stop too many trout pulling down the stalks, evenings left to the police, or the static from the tower waltzing off with our clothes, just as we swallow a frog because, as the man in the powder blue suit once put it, the bread bestowed is not anyway hard enough, when compared to the man crossing Death Valley in his freezing suit to die alone for US Gypsum, and the Knights of Leisure with their elevators in the desert happy white mound after happy white mound canceling the wave of rock outside the window; but I do question the emphasis placed on smokestack, lightning, and high sheriff given the redundancy of the World Bank or a wild fatigue shouting "fatigue" because I remember when the pass was the boss of the pass, not miles and miles the low of the window past Lancaster through Antelope Valley bringing us to the locked door or the drab wall that slurred us into existence. Now we just dance out these jitterbug embers, a habit all day like an iron wondering

perhaps there was once an innocence mistaken for Palmdale or down the road a stretch near the women's jail, a happy trail—before it was happy trails to the sex clubs on Hyperion, the pompous flux of mountain and slope that lead the elk off Bald Mountain. One does best admiring the way all of it ignores us, lest we start to prefer the dry light that scarfs up all the crumbs of this valley or the next when there is no point to rolling up your windows on my side of town—the octopus shot bland ink and the wolf is already at your door—or mine, hawking a Mayan scenario like the abdomen in the commercial even as we drag its poster all over town because when facing the carp pond the carp face you and nothing is more tedious than nostalgia or arousal——and in these parts, nostalgia is nothing but ambition set in reverse.

A STINT IN CAMARILLO OR EPISODES OF THE MAN IN THE WINDOW

Apropos the duel scene between the upholstery and your rudimental feelings,

with dried caterpillars and tannin of grasshopper,
we've prepared you a tonic
to chase the fleas off, if only

you will answer a few, brief questions—

He was pluperfect and tried to patent me, but I was too quick on
    the horn

fifteen for eleven with carbon copies the whole endeavor operating from
a swivel chair in my closet.

But in my mule orbits always thinking some days lollipops
some days coffin varnish,

                always with a turning sunward of the head,
I slide off my face.

Fat off the light hot on the front-matter
moving doublequick through the woebegone.

My choo-choo smokes a strong confetti.

It's the interior of the front, but not the foremost
that's the middle ground.

Pigs in the counting room, goats upstairs.
But I don't say nothing.

Because in my dolphin chamber, I make the substitutions
mules in the counting room, goats in the hall,

so why you always revising me? why you unzip my window?
do you defile me slowly beside Dallas?

I just don't want to dance for a living no more.

The cake of my sadness

gallops in sequins

shamelessly sweet

And molting through the streets—

          sirens in the middle ground

not the front or the foremost, the counting grounds.

The fairground had long since diminished, sprinkler flaring
and all morning the director keep crossing the yard.

I am thinking that for years I will say nothing. I will be an autistic.

But, Doctor, I don't like these walls and I must have assistance.

The man in the powder blue suit was my man, but he can't be located and I must act quickly.

And it must come from an honorable man.

But what is your rate and why is mine inferior?

Because I stare at my hands?

I want to writhe in such a way as to have an effect on others.

I mean spoke, no more spokes
smoke

I mean I want to write.

But I was sired on light, sets.

Am easily dazzled by the sound of grass

as it sets in, sets off. Hefty
sets fed on light.

Nothing overhead.

Take and attach.

Subsequently removed.

So set.

The smallest set of forces. I am their record. But if I was a sparrow
I'd spare no one.

My smallness is a sponge.

Splotches.

Squat and swallow.

Their sappy heads.

Applause.

But all morning in the window, the director keeps coming.

I don't think I could take it with nothing over my head, so light and fluffy.

Perhaps what it is like
without a brain stem.

The potato-headed surprise.

The director has a mouth like river
I sleep between his warm gums.

But in my orbit always thinkin'
some days lollipops some days sauce.

Pigs in the counting room, goats in the safe,
but I don't say nothing, and in my baths
and at my feedings, I always keep
my appointment, no matter

how gumheavy, and lagooned

and if sniffing my fingers, they smell
like gunpowder

I use a little

oil of the Grand Wazoo, dust off Aphrodite
and ride the dolphin through the aperture
left behind by the spine

ulterior to sequence

beveled light
bored a hole in this attic

to remind me of the word "doe"
heading toward formaldehyde.

But as the director says, you gots to get there somehow.

Lest the rush of freeway
lest always surrounded

lest I stare at my hands.

Doctors are not to play cards in the waiting room.

He was not to play cards here in the rooms with the customers.

He was not to be hopelessly eccentric by dedicating the manuscript to the cactus out the window.

He is simply to count out how long you are willing to dedicate yourself to the cactus outside the window.

but if you do not come to be counted

you must cherish yourself, feverishly
polish.

But what is your rate for playing cards?

What is the policy?

Is it a black paw to face, air whipping
through the harshest slits

or is like without a brainstem, maybe like Dallas?
or not saying anything for years?

or was it like maybe bubbles
on the horizon of a chin.

Another bath.

A few loving blots.

Just for staring at my hands.

LUSTER OUT OF CAMARILLO ON THE WAY TO TIJUANA

La farmacía is just a head—
the rose of euphoria is deep, keep walking
nuevas palabras nuevos mundos
pero sal si puedes
tailed by the most tenacious of feelings
that whatever is spacious is spacious forever
distance deterrence very few have made it
past the ends or fins, the glut of mines
right through the piano, constantly pounding
back and forth the endorphins coast
and the coast keeps coasting like *mal gobierno*
but in the pharmacy of love solamente nuestros
like a cosa nostra like mal gobierno
and I ain't bitter, it's just bitter sweet
ain't gonna sweat no Pinkerton
no goons no ginks no company finks
California is in the sink
and all of Cuba is Mississippi silt
so if you're dumb you better be daring
bottom's up to who's bottom first, but keep walking
I'll meet you at Dead Man's Peak.

MIDLAND: OR THE COLLEGE OF NEGLECTED SCIENCE

(*for Uncle Bob, Evan Calbi*)

Hats optional shoes forbidden, but support our troops with personal debts in the pawn shops and along the sea wall though on occasion a particular pair of waders through the quest and the question that were not, as Bob put it, in hand, just doves berserk in the compass, avuncular forms of lust, and a flirtatious hostility to remind us history was only a colon to nature despite the tedious shift of the needle from bramble to ash the peculiar slope of dignity diverging from spikes in the crime index, and a hemorrhaged clarity

Two out of three ever waltz out that caldera, and the last out is a big tarantula crawling across the angel food, up Cerro Gordo to Bob's bestiary of any opening any day it was no use, still too close to Camp Pendelton or Amalfi Drive memoirs of a critic turning over in the shore like a shoulder of ruined foam until the whole continent seemed less horse-like and more phatic—taking sides against the topsoil in Bolivia or just a few years left of gas the soft, but firm reactors over San Onofree insisting no one can escape the long worm of the lawn, as if the dirt hadn't already grown up around the music—on Red Hill.

There is nothing above the music—the rest of the week, dank serious pedestrians walking their coins, maybe five divorcés team up to dance or discuss the well-mannered illusion of technique in which shots don't exactly "ring" and the wind in the willows plays nothing particular and nothing if not partial to a lady purring thickly beneath the freeway, the beard her finest piece of jewelry, her love of pork chops something to be proud of out here where eighty-eight percent can't afford the median home. She might tells don't move, and don't peek and no one would. I never once saw the lights had gone out or the extreme tides in which words suddenly seemed to work: a man in powder blue suit lives in a powder blue world and a three-legged wolf lives in a three-legged town. This one began with a glut of blood and ends with a lack of guts but up with the scepter ahead with the athleticism even if by now the concierge can see no such population had ever existed. It had been a project of fragrance and proving things other than sixty-four cigarettes into a novel sixty-four pages until maybe sixty-four years of age, never an outsider always a reject, abrupt as Pomona or the satin whip of ellipsis, eclipse, elision after which you were gone. I returned the lake to its bowl to reflect—your project was outright rejection each day the little closet of the city nothing more than a big ole broken nose, and the ranch dressing was a tribute to half-time itself. Now it is all half-time, heat activated, if three times a week once around the block the beagle and I share the same bad knee and a plum each morning for our health, the rest of the day sleeping off the smoky red dress, and though I owned neither the helmet nor the breast plate for the occasion, I did love those debaucheries even if fabricated to keep one of us, at least, from being lonely at least then we knew why we were here—we were earthquake bait—about the best you could say was it was all worthwhile, though only for a while and only while it was—not much of a Vienna or a Rome or an Athens, but it was one hell of a Pompeii.

POST SCRIPT

"God may have made us, but John Colt made us equal."

As a way of undoing the exile which is Southern California, I've used tiny pieces here and there from the work of the following:

James Elroy, Ross McDonald: Raymond Chanlder, Joanne Kyger, John Thomas, Jack Spicer, Norma Cole, Thomas, McGrath, Martha Ronk, Frank Zappa, Dennis Phillips, Raymond Chandler, Charles Mingus, Mary Austin, Charles Bowden, Jeffrey St. Clair, Paul Vangelisti, Wesley Powell, Bob Crosson, Charles Bukowski, Bill Mohr, Neeli Cherkovski, Robinson Jeffers, Carey McWilliams, and William Mulholland. Donald Worster's beautiful ecological and social history *Rivers of Empire: Water, Aridity & the Growth of the American West* was crucially important.

Versions of many of these poems were first published as a chapbook called *Waltzing the Map* by A+Bend. I'd like to thank Jill Stengle for that. Some early versions of the Jet Propulsion Lab poems appeared in *Ribot*. A version of "From a Bear Republic" was published in *Place as Purpose*, edited by Paul Vangelisti and Martha Ronk. I would like to thank them all. And as always, a special thanks to Paris Schaefer.

Born in 1971, Standard Schaefer grew up in Houston and often traveled the landscapes of the American West in a bus with elk horns on the hood while his uncle Bob Meyer drove his summer campers around under the name "Meyer's Mountain Men." After leaving Texas for good at the age of 19, he attended college in Los Angeles where he lived in a precarious exile for 13 years while attaining a B.A. in Comparative Literature, and an MFA in writing. During that time, he became acquainted with the College of Neglected Science, particularly poets Dennis Phillips, Martha Ronk, Paul Vangelisti and Bob Crosson, the other Uncle Bob to whose memory much of this book is devoted. While in Los Angeles, he co-edited the literary journal *Rhizome* with Evan Calbi, and later *Ribot* with Paul Vangelisti. Shortly after his first book of poetry *Nova* was selected for the 1999 National Poetry Series, he learned to fly-fish and began spending more time in the Owens Valley, where the inspiration for *Water & Power* first seized him and caused him to reflect on the landscapes of his youth, the anti-Walden implications of life west of the Mississippi, and the culture industry that sustains and undermines it today. With their first child on the way, he and his wife Paris, and two beagles, Walter and Martha, have recently relocated to San Francisco, where he serves occasionally as a teacher, a free lance writer, speculator, whistle-blower, media activist, and student as well as the non-fiction editor of the *New Review of Literature.*